Minerals, Rocks, and Soil

Revised Edition

Barbara Davis

capstone

Edited by Annabel Savery
Designed by Graham Rich
Original illustrations © Discovery Books Limited 2009
Illustrated by Stefan Chabluk
Picture research by Annabel Savery

Library of Congress Cataloging-in-Publication Data is available on the Library of Congress website.
 ISBN 978-1-4109-8521-7 (revised paperback)
 ISBN 978-1-4109-8524-8 (ebook pdf)

Acknowledgements

We would like to thank the following for permission to reproduce photographs: Alamy: John Elk III, top 7, Nature Picture Library, bottom right 9, The Natural History Museum, (puddingstone) 27; Getty Images: Mark Schneider, 16; iStockphoto: 169 malcolm crooks, 43, Karen Massier, (mountains) 20-21, mikeuk, bottom right 21, robas, 11, tracy tucker, 41; Newscom: Dorling Kindersley Universal Images Group, bottom right 6, TPG Top Photo Group, 42; Shutterstock: Aaron Amat, (marble) 34, Adam J, top 31, Ahuli Labutin, 17, Albert Russ, bottom middle 6, (fluorite) 15, bottom left 19, Andrew Kerr, (quartzite)34, Bjoern Wylezich, (diamond) 15, Brian Kinney, 32, Cagla Acikgoz, 4, Dorn1530, (sandstone) 27, top left 34, Enki Photo, bottom right 23, Feem PT, top 27, Frontpage, 25, Gerardo C.Lerner, bottom 35, Giovanna Di Mauro, (calcite) 15, Joe Goodson, (limestone) 34, josefauer, top 9, Joshua Haviv, design element throughout, top 29, top left 30, Kelsey Green, 24, Lizard, 36, Love Silhouette, (copper wire) 15, MarcelClemens, (pyrite) 15, Michael Effler, 38, Mirka Moksha, bottom 7, Nastya22, top left 19, Nickolay Vinokurov, bottom 30-31, nmiskovic, 28, Noam Armonn, 40, Ocskay Bence, top right 23, Only Fabrizio, 18, panpilas Lertpunyaroj, cover, Parmna, (shale) 27, Patricia Chumillas, (crystals) bottom right cover, Paul Maguire, (fossil) 29, Peeradach Rattanakoses, (rings) 15, Rich Carey, 33, Richard Peterson, (apatite) 15, Sashkin, (paint cans) 13, Sementer, bottom left 6, Somchai Som, (light bulb) 13, Stefano Cavoretto, (quartz) 15, STILLFX, (toaster) 13, StockStudio, (cars) 13, V.Borisov, (watch) 13, Vadim Petrakov, top 35, Ververidis Vasilis, 3, 12, vvoe, (talc) 15, (corundum) 15, middle left 19, yanatul, (battries) 13, Zbynek Burival, (gypsum) 15, (feldspar) 15, Zelenskaya, (topaz) 15

We would like to thank content consultant Suzy Gazlay and text consultant Nancy Harris for their invaluable help in the preparation of this book.
Every effort has been made to contact copyright holders of material reproduced in this book. Any omissions will be rectified in subsequent printings if notice is given to the publishers.
All the Internet addresses (URLs) given in this book were valid at the time of going to press. However, due to the dynamic nature of the Internet, some addresses may have changed, or sites may have changed or ceased to exist since publication. While the author and Publishers regret any inconvenience this may cause readers, no responsibility for any such changes can be accepted by either the author or the Publishers.

Contents

Why is titanium used to make special wheelchairs? Find out on page 12!

How do living creatures become fossils? Find out on page 29!

Some words are shown in bold, **like this.** These words are explained in the glossary. You will find important information and definitions underlined, **like this.**

A WORLD OF MINERALS, ROCKS, AND SOIL

Did you know that you are surrounded by minerals, rocks, and soil? You might be walking through a town with buildings towering over you. You could be strolling in a park, or walking down a road lined with cars. Wherever you are, minerals, rocks, and soil are all around you.

The buildings might be made from rocks, such as granite and limestone. The green grass in the park grows in soil. The cars are made from steel. Steel is made from the metal iron, which comes from the mineral hematite.

Minerals come in an exciting variety of shapes and colors. These crystals are formed from the minerals quartz, sphalerite, and golden pyrite.

What is a mineral?

There are more than 3,000 different types of minerals. All minerals contain one or more **elements**. They are found all over Earth, though some are much more common than others. Some minerals are found within rocks, and some are found on their own. A substance must have the five characteristics below to be **classified** as a mineral.

Naturally occurring	Inorganic	Solid	Crystal structure	Definite chemical composition
A mineral is made naturally in the ground. It is not made by human beings.	A mineral is not formed of any material that was once a living thing or part of a living thing.	A mineral is always found as a **solid**. It cannot exist in nature as a **liquid** or **gas**.	A mineral is made of **particles** (tiny pieces) that are grouped together in a pattern. The pattern is called a **crystal structure**.	A mineral has a definite chemical composition. Each mineral is made of one or more elements that are always in the same proportions. For example, each **molecule** of halite contains one sodium **atom** and one chlorine atom joined together.

Common Elements

There are more than 100 known elements. Out of these, oxygen, silicon, aluminum, iron, calcium, sodium, potassium, and magnesium are the most common in Earth's **crust**. These eight elements combine with each other, and other elements, in different ways to form every kind of mineral.

How minerals form

Minerals form through the process of making crystals. This is called **crystallization**. During this process, the particles of a mineral line up in a pattern. The pattern repeats itself over and over again. This forms a solid called a **crystal**. A crystal has flat sides that meet at sharp corners. The flat sides are called **faces**.

Crystal structures

Each mineral has a particular crystal structure. The structure is described by the number of faces and the types of angles formed. Quartz crystal, for example, has six faces. A magnetite crystal (usually) has eight faces.

Crystals can be many different shapes. The shapes are grouped into crystal systems that describe the number, size, and shape of the crystal's surfaces.

Below are some examples of crystal systems.

 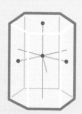    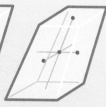

Isometric   **Hexagonal**   **Tetragonal**   **Orthorhombic**   **Monoclinic**   **Triclinic**

Monoclinic—orthoclase   **Orthorhombic—barite**   **Triclinic—amblygonite**

Forming crystals

Mineral crystals form in one of two ways. They can form when the liquid **evaporates** from a **solution**. Seawater is a solution. It contains the mineral halite. When the water in seawater evaporates, the **dissolved** halite forms into crystals. Halite is also called rock salt.

Halite crystal formations in Death Valley, California.

Mineral crystals also form when molten (melted) materials harden. Below Earth's crust (uppermost layer) is a layer of hot, molten rock called **magma**. The molten rock contains minerals. When the magma cools the minerals form into crystals and they become a solid.

The mineral labradorite forms when molten rock hardens.

GROWING HAND CRYSTALS
Growing salt crystals is fun and easy to do!

What you need

- Epsom salts
- Table salt
- Water
- 2 shallow dishes
- Measuring cup
- Black construction paper
- Magnifying glass

What you do

- Mix a cup of Epsom salts with three cups of water in a shallow dish.
- Mix a cup of table salt with three cups of water in another shallow dish.
- Lay a large piece of the black construction paper on a table or other flat surface.
- Place one hand in each dish. Shake your hands to get rid of excess water. Place you palms down side by side on the construction paper.
- Wash and dry your hands.
- Let the palm prints dry for several hours or overnight.
- Use a magnifying glass to look closely at the crystals formed by the Epsom salts and the table salt.

OUCH ALERT!
Do not do this experiment if you have an open cut on your hand. Salt in an open cut will sting!

FINDING AND USING MINERALS

Earth's **crust** is made almost entirely of **minerals**. There are about 3,700 known minerals found in Earth's crust. New minerals are being discovered all the time.

All over the world

Minerals are found all over the world. Some areas have greater amounts of certain minerals because of the way in which Earth developed over millions of years. The mineral halite, known as rock salt, is found in areas that were once covered in oceans. Mountains and volcanoes have rich deposits of minerals containing **elements**, such as iron, copper, cobalt, and manganese.

Minerals can be found all over the world. This map shows where major deposits of some important minerals are found.

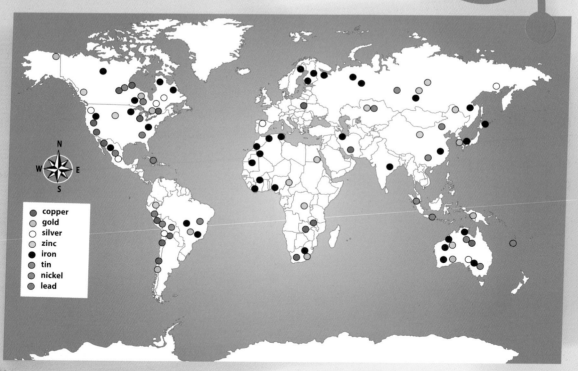

- copper
- gold
- silver
- zinc
- iron
- tin
- nickel
- lead

Metals and ores

Metals are elements, but they are not usually found in nature in their pure form. Metals are found mixed up with other elements and minerals in an **ore**. An ore is a rock that contains a metal or a valuable mineral. For example, iron is a common metal. It is taken out of the mineral ore hematite.

Ore is removed from the ground to extract the metals and minerals it contains.

MINERALS IN THE OCEAN

The ocean floor has mineral deposits that contain valuable elements, such as manganese, nickel, copper, iron, cobalt, and platinum. Large **mining** ships use advanced technology to locate these mineral deposits. They use special equipment, such as a remote robot, that can scoop up samples of ocean floor. The robot sends the sample through a long tube up to the waiting ship. There, the sample is inspected in the hope of finding valuable minerals.

This remote robot is used to collect mineral samples.

Mining

Before minerals and metals can be used, the ore must be dug out of the ground. Mining is a way to **extract**, or remove, ore from the ground. It is a vast industry and, because metals and minerals are valuable, can be very profitable. Different types of mines are used depending on the type of ore. <u>**There are three types of mines: shaft mines, strip mines, and open-pit mines.**</u>

Trucks remove ore from an open-pit copper mine in the Atacama Desert in northern Chile. Open-pit and strip mines can cause lasting damage to the land.

Shaft mines

A shaft mine contains a series of tunnels that are dug deep into the ground. These types of mines are needed to find ores containing **mineral veins** (minerals that have crystallized in cracks in rock), such as silver.

Strip mines

In strip mines heavy equipment is used to strip away layers of **soil** until the ore is found. Strip mining is often used for minerals that are close to the surface.

Open-pit mines

An open-pit mine is a huge hole in the ground that goes down many hundreds of meters. Miners use giant earth-moving equipment to scoop out soil and rock. Open-pit mines are often used for ores that are close to the surface but may also be found deeper in the ground.

ENVIRONMENTAL IMPACT OF MINING

Mining for minerals and metals can harm the environment. Waste materials from mining can pollute water supplies and soil. Strip and open-pit mining can involve chopping down acres of trees and cutting deep holes that scar the land. Some governments now require mine operators to restore land damaged by mining.

Using minerals

Look in the window of a jewelry store and you will see a display of sparkling gemstones. Gold rings seem to glow and precious stones twinkle in the window lights. For thousands of years, people have prized certain minerals for their rarity and beauty. These are the famous gems like diamonds, rubies, and emeralds that almost anyone can recognize.

USEFUL METAL

The metal titanium is particularly strong and very light. These properties make it very popular for building special wheelchairs for racing or for playing basketball.

Minerals in the Home

Although they are the best-known, gemstones are not the most important minerals. Think about the things in your home. How many are made from minerals?

The metal zinc is used in batteries. It is found in the mineral sphalerite.

The thin filament wire in a lightbulb is made of tungsten, a metal often found in the mineral ore scheelite.

The inside of a toaster is usually made with aluminum. This metal is usually found in the mineral bauxite.

The frames of vehicles, such as cars and buses, are made from steel. Iron is used to make steel. Iron is found in several minerals including hematite and magnetite.

A powdered form of titanium is used in paint. Titanium is a metal found in the minerals ilmenite and rutile.

Quartz is used in watches, communication equipment, and computers. Quartz is one of the most common minerals on Earth.

Identifying Minerals

Each mineral has certain properties that can be used to identify it. A **property** is a particular feature of the mineral, such as how it looks or how easily it breaks. Scientists look at eight basic properties to help them identify different minerals. These are: **hardness,** color, **streak,** luster, **density,** crystal system, **cleavage** and **fracture,** and special properties.

HARDNESS

One of the best clues to a mineral's identity is how easily it can scratch something else or be scratched itself. This is a measure of its hardness. Talc is one of the softest minerals. It can be scratched with a fingernail. The talcum powder you may have at home is made from talc that has been ground into a powder. Diamond is the hardest mineral. Diamonds are so hard that they can only be scratched by another diamond.

BREAKING MINERALS

Hardness does not describe how easily a mineral can be broken. As hard as diamonds are, they can be broken apart.

MOHS' HARDNESS SCALE

Friedrich Mohs was born in 1773 in Germany. In 1812, he developed a way to compare the hardness of common minerals. Mohs' hardness scale rates the hardness of minerals on a scale of 1 to 10. A mineral will be able to scratch all other minerals with lower numbers than its own.

MINERAL	HARDNESS RATING	EXAMPLES OF HARDNESS RATINGS
Talc	1	
Gypsum	2	Fingernail—2.5 Gold and silver—2.5 to 3
Calcite	3	Copper wire—3
Fluorite	4	Platinum—4 to 4.5
Apatite	5	Common knife blade—5.5
Feldspar (also called orthoclase)	6	Iron pyrite—6.5
Quartz	7	Glass—6 to 7
Topaz	8	Hardened steel file—7+
Corundum	9	
Diamond	10	

COLOR

Some minerals are always the same color. Azurite can be identified because it is always blue. Malachite is always green. However, most minerals cannot be identified just by color. Quartz and fluorite, for example, come in many colors.

Luster

Luster describes the way a mineral reflects light. Minerals can have **metallic** luster. Their surfaces look like polished metal. Some minerals look like pieces of hard candy that have been sucked. Scientists say these have a "gumdrop luster." Other luster terms are dull, earthy, greasy, silky, and waxy.

STREAK

When a mineral is scraped against a special, unglazed tile called a streak plate it leaves a powder behind. This is called its streak. A mineral's streak color is often different from the mineral's color. Hematite can be black, dark red, or silver in color. Its powder, though, is always a dark red-brown.

This streak test shows that gray magnetite has black powder.

Pencils

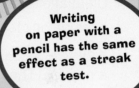

Graphite is a very soft mineral that leaves a streak even on paper. Graphite is used in pencils.

Writing on paper with a pencil has the same effect as a streak test.

DENSITY

Density is the mass of an object in a given space, or volume. If you held two mineral samples of equal size in your hands, the mineral with the higher density would feel heavier. Scientists measure the mass of an object with a balance scale. They then measure the volume of the same object. For example, if an object is a cube it would be measured by its dimensions. Density is the mass of the object divided by the volume of the object. It is expressed in a numerical value, such as grams per cubic centimeter (g/cm^3).

Crystal System

Each mineral has its own **crystal structure** (see pages 6 and 7). For example, halite **crystals** have six faces that meet at right angles and form a perfect cube. The crystal system for halite is cubic.

CLEAVAGE AND FRACTURE

- Cleavage describes a mineral that breaks, or cleaves, easily along a smooth, flat surface. Mica is a mineral that has cleavage. It breaks into separate flat sheets.

- A mineral that breaks with uneven or rough surfaces is said to have fracture. This term is also used to describe the way a fracture looks. For example, quartz looks like seashell when broken open, so it has a shell fracture.

SPECIAL PROPERTIES

Some minerals have unique properties that can be used to help identify them.

- Magnetite is magnetic.
- Calcite fizzes when hydrochloric acid is poured on it.
- Scheelite glows under **ultraviolet light.**

Copper forms jagged points when it is broken, so it is said to have a hackly (spiky) fracture.

COMPARING MINERAL PROPERTIES

Azurite, magnetite, and quartz are different types of minerals. The table below gives information about their properties.

Mineral	Hardness	Color	Luster	Streak	Density (g/cm³)	Special properties, cleavage, and fracture
Azurite	3 ½—4	Blue	Dull, earthy, or glassy	Pale blue	3.8	Fizzes and dissolves when in contact with hydrochloric acid.
Magnetite	6	Black or dark gray	Metallic	Black	5.2	Magnetic
Quartz	7	Clear (transparent) or a range of colors	Glassy	No color	2.6	Fracture—like broken glass.

Density quick check: Assume that you have samples of all the three minerals listed above. The samples are all the same size. Which mineral do you think would feel the heaviest in your palm?

Find the answer on page 47!

WHAT IS A ROCK?

A rock is a mixture of one or more minerals found in nature. There are three main kinds of rocks found on Earth—**igneous, sedimentary,** and **metamorphic.** Each kind of rock forms in a different way. The names of the three kinds of rocks describe how the rocks are formed.

Taking a closer look

You're walking along a beach when you see an interesting-looking pink stone. Picking it up, you notice that it feels rough and has little flecks of black on its surface. The sunlight catches the stone and it seems to sparkle.

You look at it closely with a hand lens. Then, you put on safety glasses, take a small hammer and break off a part of the stone to see what it looks like inside. You may not know it, but you have just done some of the tests a **geologist** would do to **classify** an unknown rock. From tests like these you can find out what type of rock it is and how it formed.

Mountains can be made of igneous, sedimentary, or metamorphic rock. Many mountains are made of a combination of types of rocks.

ROCKS IN YOUR WORLD

Take a walk with family or friends to see how many ways rocks are used in your neighborhood.

WHAT YOU NEED:

- small notebook
- pencil or pen
- magnifying glass

WHAT YOU DO:

1 Write down all the different uses for rocks that you see during your walk. Look for buildings, statues, walls, and anything else made of rock.

2 Look very closely at each rock you find. Try to describe it, using as much detail as possible. Here are some questions you might want to ask yourself about the rock you are examining:

- Where did I find the rock? Are similar rocks nearby?

- What color is the rock? (Describe different shades, striping, and flecks of color.)

- Is the rock smooth or rough or a combination of textures?

- Does the rock look like it has been fractured?

- Has the rock been polished or cut in some way?

A geologist would take careful notes of their observations for later reference. You can, too!

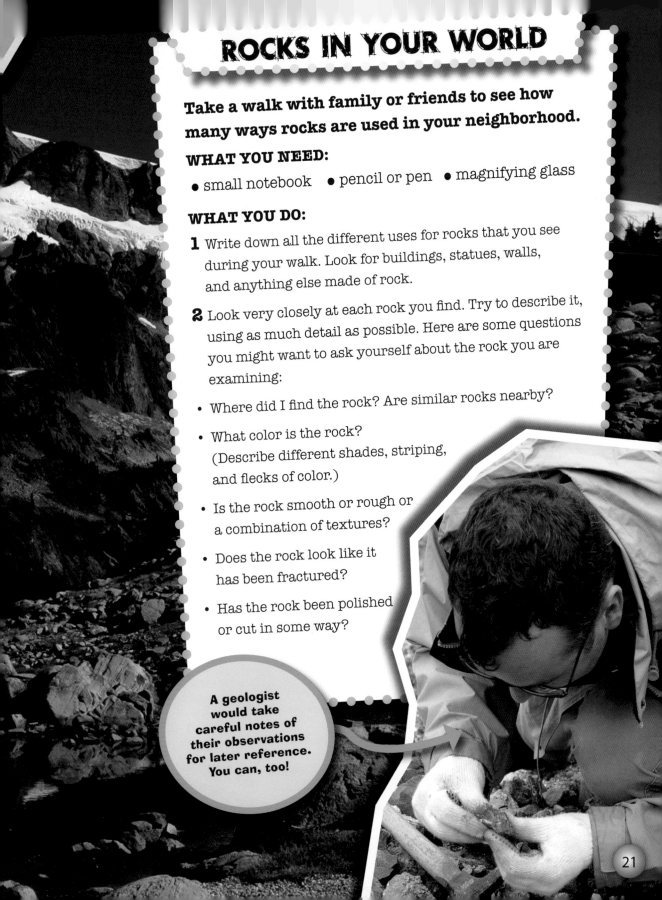

Igneous Rocks

From the top of the mountain the telltale smoke puffs into the sky. The smoke becomes denser. Then, the volcano erupts! Hot **lava** flows down the side of the mountain.

The lava is molten rock that started out deep inside the volcano as **magma**. When this molten rock cools, it becomes **igneous rock**. Over time, layers of cooled igneous rock will build up to form the volcanic mountain.

Science Word Clue

When you think of igneous rock, think of rock formed from fire—like the fire from a volcano. *"Igneous"* comes from the Latin word *"ignis,"* meaning *"fire."* The English word, *"ignite,"* comes from that same Latin word.

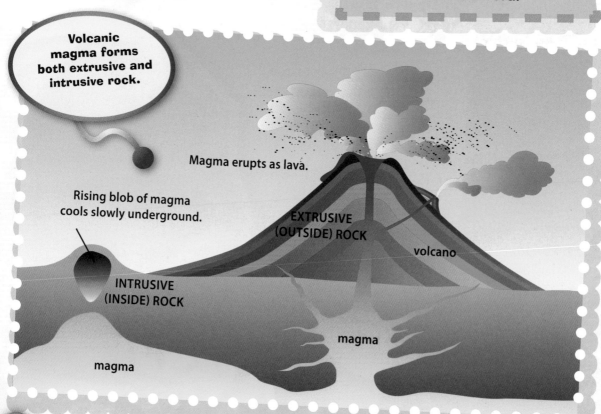

Volcanic magma forms both extrusive and intrusive rock.

Magma erupts as lava.

Rising blob of magma cools slowly underground.

EXTRUSIVE (OUTSIDE) ROCK

volcano

INTRUSIVE (INSIDE) ROCK

magma

magma

Inside or outside

Igneous rock can form above or below Earth's surface. Igneous rock that forms when lava cools above Earth's surface is called **extrusive rock**. The most common extrusive rock is called basalt. A large part of Earth's **crust** is made of basalt, including the crust beneath the ocean floor.

Extrusive rock cools quickly as the temperature above Earth's surface is much colder than below it. The **crystals** form quickly and so are smaller. This gives extrusive rock a smoother surface.

Intrusive rock is igneous rock that forms when magma cools below Earth's surface. Intrusive rocks cool more slowly than extrusive rocks. This allows larger crystals to form, which makes intrusive rocks coarse or rough. Granite is the most common type of intrusive rock. It is the part of Earth's crust that forms the continents and the mountains that sit on them. Many mountains have granite cores (centers).

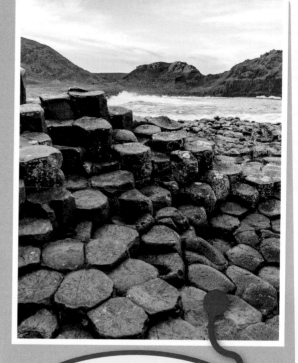

The Giant's Causeway in County Antrim, Northern Ireland is made of about 40,000 basalt rock columns.

Obsidian has smooth, glass-like surfaces because no crystals have formed.

Uses of igneous rocks

People throughout history have used igneous rock for building materials and tools. Granite is one of the most plentiful igneous rocks. The ancient Egyptians used granite to build temples and to carve giant statues of their kings and queens. Ancient Native Americans used obsidian to make sharp-edged knives and other tools for cutting or scraping animal skins.

In South America, the Incas of Peru used granite and other igneous rocks to build a great **fortress** near the present-day city of Cuzco.

The faces of four U.S. presidents are carved in the granite of Mount Rushmore in South Dakota.

Igneous rocks today

Igneous rocks are still used in important ways. Basalt is crushed into small pieces to make gravel that is used for roads. Granite is cut into sheets, polished, and used for floors and kitchen surfaces. Granite is still a popular choice for modern office buildings and public places.

ROCKS IN THE KITCHEN

Pumice is an igneous rock that is used as an **abrasive**. It can scratch or peel away other softer materials. Pumice is ground into a fine powder and added to kitchen cleaning and polishing products.

SEDIMENTARY ROCKS

Sediment is small, loose pieces of material that come from rocks, minerals, and living things. <u>Sedimentary rocks form when layers of sediment are pressed and then stick together.</u> Read on to find out more!

How Sedimentary Rocks Form

Sedimentary **rocks** form in three stages:
1. Wind, water, ice, and gravity move sediment from one place and **deposit** it in another.

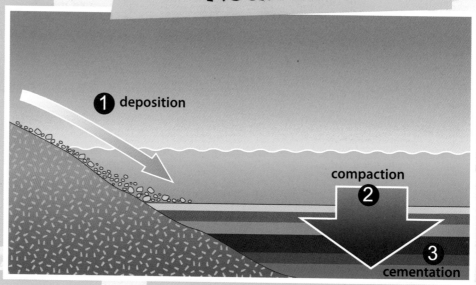

1 deposition

compaction **2**

3 cementation

2. Over millions of years, layers of sediment build up. The heavy layers begin to press down on one another. This is called **compaction**.

3. While the layers are compacting, the minerals in the rock begin to **dissolve** in the water trapped in the layers. These minerals slowly flow in between the sediment and act like glue to bind together, or cement, the sediment **particles**. This is called **cementation**.

Telling stories

Sedimentary rocks can tell stories about how and where they formed. The stories include what the weather was like. Sandstone will show ripples like water does when the wind blows across its surface. This tells scientists that wind or water was pushing the sandstone while the layer was forming.

Sandstone arches, like this one in Arches National Park, Utah, took millions of years to form.

COMBINING ROCKS

Most sedimentary rocks are made up of pieces of other rocks. Some pieces can be so small you can't see them without a microscope. Other pieces are so large, a human being couldn't move them.

Type of sedimentary rock	Type of rock particles
 **Sandstone**	Small fragments of sand.
 **Pudding stone**	Small and large rock fragments with smooth, rounded edges. These types of rocks are called conglomerates.
 **Shale**	Tiny particles of clay.

Rocks from living things

Some types of sedimentary rock are not formed from other rocks. **Organic rock** is formed from the remains of living things. Limestone forms from the shells and skeletons of sea creatures, such as shellfish, fish, and coral. When the animals die, their shells and bones fall to the ocean floor as sediment. Layers of this sediment build over millions of years creating limestone deposits that can be many hundreds of meters deep.

At one time, seawater covered the giant limestone cliffs of this Greek island.

Coal

Coal forms when pieces of dead swamp plants are buried in layers with other sediments. Gradually, microscopic living things change the **chemicals** in the plants. Over millions of years, the layers go through compaction to form coal. Many people believe that coal is a mineral, but it is not. Minerals are not formed from the remains of living things.

Limestone Caves

As rainwater seeps through the ground it absorbs carbon dioxide from the soil. The water and the carbon dioxide (CO_2) mix to form a very weak acid called carbonic acid. This acid slowly wears away limestone deposits. Caves form when the rock is dissolved away over many years.

Some limestone caves have been used for thousands of years as burial sites. The Diros caves in Greece, for example, were used as burial sites during the late Neolithic and Early Bronze Ages (3500 to 2500 BCE).

There are many examples of dramatic and beautiful caves formed from limestone deposits.

SKELETON ROCK!

Chalk is a type of limestone. When you use chalk to write or draw pictures, you're using the skeletons of microscopic creatures that once lived in oceans!

Fossils

A **fossil** is the remains of a living thing. Fossils form when an animal or plant dies and the remains are quickly buried by sediment. Living things have minerals in their bodies. Over a long period of time, these minerals dissolve. They are replaced by the minerals in the sediment. The result is a copy of whatever was buried.

Fossils help scientists learn about the plants and animals that lived on Earth millions of years ago.

Using sedimentary rocks

Sedimentary rocks are used in many different ways. Some are used in building. Limestone is used to make cement, and shale is used to make bricks. Other sedimentary rocks are used to create **energy**.

Houses of sand

Sandstone has been used in some of the world's most famous and beautiful buildings. The White House, in Washington, D.C., was built with a type of sandstone that easily absorbs water.

To prevent water damage, the craftsmen that built the White House painted the walls with a protective coating. The coating dried to a white color, giving the White House its name.

ROCK ENERGY

Coal burns easily and is an important source of energy. It takes a long time to form, though. Many scientists are concerned that the world will run out of coal. Scientists all over the world are studying ways to replace coal with other sources of energy.

Coal is a type of sedimentary rock that takes millions of years to form. This is why it is called a "nonrenewable" energy source.

CHEMICAL ROCKS

Some sedimentary rocks are called chemical rocks. These are rocks that form when seas or lakes **evaporate**. Gypsum is a chemical rock that forms when seawater evaporates. It is used in plaster of Paris for surgical **splints** and casting molds. Gypsum is also used as a fertilizer and soil conditioner.

When the water from the Dead Sea evaporates, it leaves behind large deposits of salt, gypsum, potash, and other chemicals.

CORAL REEFS

Coral reefs provide food and shelter for many sea animals.

Coral animals live in the warm waters of tropical seas. Most are only about the size of a fingernail. Some are even smaller. Coral animals are in the same family as jellyfish. Unlike jellyfish, coral animals grow outer skeletons made of calcite.

Coral skeletons

Billions of coral skeletons grow together and form a coral reef. When the coral animals die, their skeletons remain behind. New coral animals build on these skeletons. Over time, a coral reef can stretch for hundreds of kilometers. It becomes home to many other living things, from sea anemones to fish.

Global warming

Coral reefs face a threat from **global warming**. Increases in water temperatures upset the balance among the creatures of the reef. The coral itself begins to die off. The other reef animals lose their food and shelter. Some reefs can recover, but many are disappearing. Scientists are trying to find ways to protect the world's coral reefs and help the oceans stay healthy.

When coral dies off, it can no longer support other sea animals.

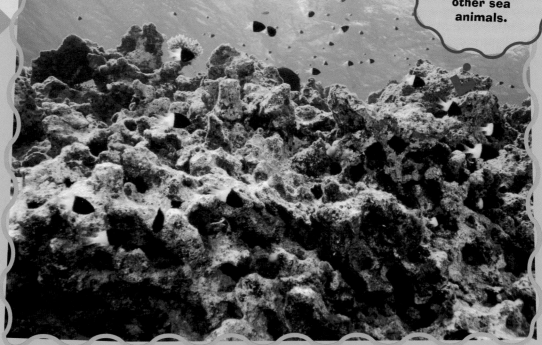

Limestone uncovered

The **organic rock** limestone comes from ancient coral reefs. Millions of years ago, there were vast saltwater oceans covering most of Earth. As Earth has changed over time oceans have become smaller. **Fossils** and massive layers of limestone that were covered by the sea have been exposed.

Metamorphic Rocks

Metamorphic rock is rock that has changed from one type to another.

As rock layers build, the lower layers are squashed and put under lots of pressure. This pressure creates heat. Extreme heat and pressure change the minerals in a rock into different minerals. The rock's appearance also changes. With these changes, the rock itself becomes a different type of rock. **Igneous** or **sedimentary** rock can change into **metamorphic** rock.

Sandstone (sedimentary) → Quartzite (metamorphic)

Limestone (sedimentary) → Marble (metamorphic)

Changing form

Rocks can change more than once. One type of metamorphic rock can re-form into another type. For example, shale is a sedimentary rock that can become slate, a metamorphic rock. Slate can then change into phyllite, another metamorphic rock.

SCIENCE WORD CLUE

The word "metamorphic" comes from two Greek words. *Meta* means "change." *Morphosis* means "form." So, a metamorphic rock is one that has "changed form."

Mountains and monuments

The Rocky Mountains in North America, the Alps in Europe, and the Himalayas in Asia are all examples of mountains formed from metamorphic rock. These mountain ranges formed when forces beneath Earth's surface caused large areas of land to crash together. The rock was squeezed and folded. Metamorphic rock that had formed deep within Earth's **crust** was pushed up to form mountains.

It takes millions of years for mountains to form. During that time, rocks often change from one type to another.

The Palacio de Bellas Artes in Mexico City is made of white marble from Italy. It was begun in 1904 and took 30 years to build.

Long-lasting

The heat and pressure that metamorphic rocks go through makes them very hard and **durable.** Artists and builders often choose to make their sculptures and monuments from metamorphic rock because they want their work to last for hundreds or thousands of years.

THE ROCK CYCLE

Earth's rocks are changing all the time. <u>Forces inside and on Earth's surface build, break down, and change the rocks of Earth's crust.</u> This slow and never-ending process is called the **rock cycle**. You can see how the rocks move and change in the diagram on the opposite page. Weathering and erosion are important parts of the process.

Weathering and erosion

Weathering and erosion wear away rocks and create the **sediment** that will gradually form another rock.

As wind and rain lash against rocks, tiny pieces are broken off. Rain also runs into cracks in rocks and then freezes in the cold weather. Water expands as it freezes, so the cracks are made bigger. Eventually the rock breaks apart. This is the process of weathering.

As the broken pieces of rock fall and bump against each other, tiny pieces break off, and gradually the pieces get smaller.

As rivers and **glaciers** travel over rocks they carry the small rocks with them rubbing and bumping them against each other. This process is called erosion.

Weathering and erosion are constantly breaking down the rocks that make up mountains.

Always changing

A rock cycle can follow many different paths. For example, sediment may build up over millions of years to form **sedimentary rock**. Earth's forces push the rock deep beneath the surface where the pressure and heat are extreme. The sedimentary rock becomes **metamorphic rock**. This rock then melts and is pushed to the surface as **lava**. The lava cools to become **igneous rock**. Weathering and erosion slowly wear away igneous rock. Its **particles** may be carried to a river where they settle as sediment on the river bottom. Millions of years pass, layers form, and the particles become a new sedimentary rock. Then that rock will continue to move through the rock cycle.

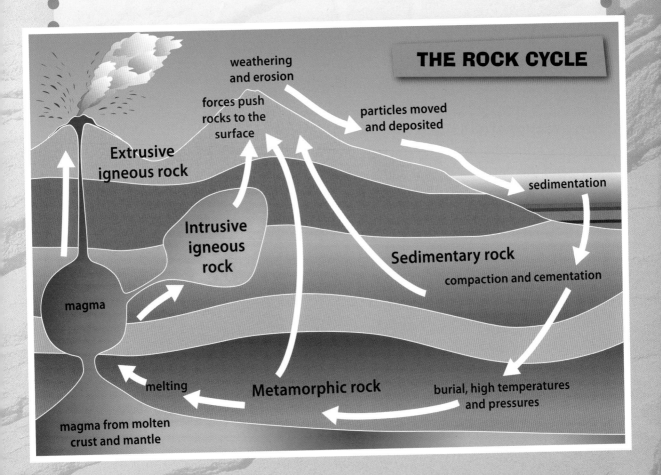

THE ROCK CYCLE

weathering and erosion

forces push rocks to the surface

particles moved and deposited

Extrusive igneous rock

sedimentation

Intrusive igneous rock

Sedimentary rock

compaction and cementation

magma

melting

Metamorphic rock

burial, high temperatures and pressures

magma from molten crust and mantle

WHAT IS SOIL?

Everything that lives on land depends on soil in one way or another. Most plants need soil to grow. Plants are the first food source for millions of living things. Healthy soil means healthy plants.

Grazing animals, such as cows, need good grass to eat. The better the soil, the better the grass.

Soil from rock

Soil is a mixture of rock **particles**, **minerals**, air, water, and the decayed remains of living things. Bedrock is the solid layer of rock found beneath the loose particles that form soil. When bedrock is exposed, **weathering** and **erosion** break the rock down into smaller and smaller particles. These particles are the basic materials of soil.

Soil Horizons

Soil forms over a long period of time. It slowly develops layers that are different in color and texture. Each of these layers is called a **soil horizon**. Scientists **classify** soil into three horizons. These are partly-weathered bedrock, **subsoil**, and **topsoil**. Plants grow in the topsoil. They need the right mixture of materials to thrive, especially a substance called **humus**. This is organic material that forms from decaying plants and animals.

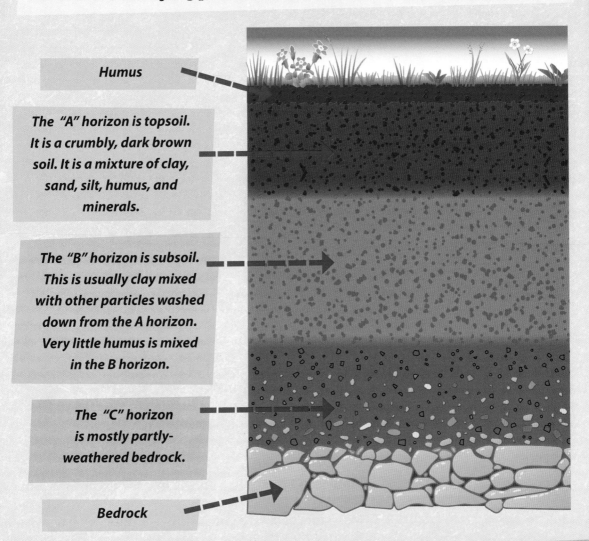

Humus

The "A" horizon is topsoil. It is a crumbly, dark brown soil. It is a mixture of clay, sand, silt, humus, and minerals.

The "B" horizon is subsoil. This is usually clay mixed with other particles washed down from the A horizon. Very little humus is mixed in the B horizon.

The "C" horizon is mostly partly-weathered bedrock.

Bedrock

Types of soil

In most soil, the rock particles are a mixture of sand, **silt**, and clay. Sand feels coarse and has the largest particles. Silt is a type of **sediment** of mud or clay that is deposited at the bottom of a river or lake. Its particle size is between that of sand and clay. Clay is smooth. It has the smallest particles. The amount of each of these particles in soil affects the soil's **texture**. The texture affects how well plants grow in a particular type of soil.

Plants thrive in good soil.

Take a close look at soil and see what you can find!

WHAT YOU NEED:

- magnifying glass
- a sheet of white paper
- a spoon of soil from around your school or home
- notepaper
- pen or pencil

WHAT YOU DO:

Spread out the spoon of soil on the sheet of paper. Look at it closely with the hand lens.

Try to identify the types of particles in the soil. Look for sand, clay, or loam (see page 41).

Rub a bit of soil between your fingers. Does it feel gritty or smooth?

Write down what you think the ingredients are in the soil.

Make sure you wash your hands well once you have finished the activity.

SAND

Sand particles are so large that the soil barely holds water at all. Water tends to quickly drain through. There is plenty of air for the plant, but it dies because it can't get enough water.

CLAY

Soil that is mostly clay will be dense and heavy. Some clay soils hold a lot of water but don't have many pockets of air. Plants in clay soil can "drown" because of this lack of air.

LOAM

Loam is made up of nearly equal parts of clay, sand, and silt. It has a crumbly texture instead of being coarse or smooth. This texture helps it hold the right amounts of both water and air. Most plants grow best in loam.

Soil conservation

Soil is one of Earth's most valuable **resources**. It can form wherever rock weathers. Soil takes a long time to form, though. It can take hundreds of years to build up just a few centimeters of soil. Areas that are good for farming have rich loam that has taken thousands of years to develop.

Only one-eighth of the land on Earth is good for farming. Using the right farming methods is very important in protecting valuable soil. Some methods disturb as little of the topsoil as possible. Dried weeds or the remains of last year's crop are left in the fields. They will act to hold the soil in place. This helps prevent erosion while also returning **nutrients** to the soil.

Desertification is the name given to the process that changes good farming soil to dry dust.

TURNING FARM FIELDS TO DESERTS

Wind erosion can cause major soil loss. Decades of drought in Africa have dried out topsoil. The farming methods used for generations did not protect the soil during periods of little rainfall. The soil is turning to dust and blowing away. This means that crops cannot grow and little food can be produced. Many scientists believe that large areas that were once fertile growing areas are now lost.

Farmers need to think carefully and plan how to use their land so that they protect valuable resources.

Conserving resources

Many places on Earth are rich in mineral and soil resources. However, valuable mineral deposits such as manganese, iron, copper, and nickel can be mined to the point that the deposits are used up. Soil can also be overused and degraded.

It is important to use resources wisely. Most countries now take action to use mining methods that are not wasteful. People are encouraged to recycle many metals, such as iron and copper. Soil **conservation** has become a life or death issue for many places in the world. Taking care of Earth's resources will make sure they can be enjoyed by future generations.

SUMMARY QUIZ

Now try this fun quiz to test what you have learned about **minerals**, rocks, and **soil!** Turn to page 47 for the answers.

1. **Metamorphic rock** is rock that
   a. has a shiny surface.
   b. has changed from another type of rock.
   c. is built from layers of sand **particles**.
   d. cracks easily.

2. Testing to see how easily a mineral can scratch something else or be scratched itself is a test of the mineral's
   a. luster.
   b. **density.**
   c. **crystal structure.**
   d. **hardness.**

3. Minerals form through the process of
   a. **crystallization.**
   b. **sedimentation.**
   c. **weathering.**
   d. the movement of **glaciers.**

4. Terms like gumdrop, earthy, greasy, and silky describe a mineral's
   a. **streak.**
   b. color.
   c. luster.
   d. hardness.

5. A rock that forms when molten rock cools is
   a. **igneous.**
   b. metamorphic.
   c. **sedimentary.**
   d. an **ore.**

6. The second stage in the formation of sedimentary rock is
   a. **compaction.**
   b. **deposit.**
   c. **cementation.**
   d. **erosion.**

7. The never-ending process that causes rocks to be built, changed, and destroyed is called
   a. weathering.
   b. erosion.
   c. the **rock cycle**.
   d. the water cycle.

8. One of the most common types of sedimentary rock is
   a. granite.
   b. quartz.
   c. hematite.
   d. sandstone.

9. Minerals are found
   a. only on the ocean floor.
   b. all over the world.
   c. only in mines.
   d. only in dried riverbeds.

10. A mine that uses a series of tunnels dug deep into the ground is called
    a. a shaft mine.
    b. an open-pit mine.
    c. a strip mine.
    d. a cave mine.

Glossary

abrasive rough, able to grind away other materials

atom the smallest part of a substance

cementation the process through which sediment particles are glued together

chemical a substance that has special properties

classify to identify something by its properties and characteristics

cleavage a mineral property of splitting or breaking along a flat surface

coal an organic rock that forms from the remains of plants

compaction the process of particles being squashed together

conservation preservation and protection of natural resources

crust the outermost layer of Earth that is made of rock

crystal a solid formed from particles arranged in a repeating pattern

crystal structure the way in which the particles in a mineral are arranged

crystallization the process of crystals forming

density the mass of an object in a given space

deposit (verb) to leave particles of sediment, minerals, or sand

dissolve to mix a solid into a liquid

durable able to last a long time; will not be easily worn away or broken down

element a substance made of just one kind of atom

energy power from coal or other sources that makes machines work or provides heat

erosion the breaking down of rocks through the action of water, wind, and glaciers

evaporate to change from a liquid into a vapor

extract to take one substance out of another

extrusive rock igneous rock that forms when lava cools above Earth's surface

face the flat side of a crystal

fortress a structure built to protect against attacks

fossil the remains of a living thing that has been buried and over time has become a rock

fracture a mineral property of breaking apart with uneven or rough surfaces

gas a substance in which the particles are widely spread out; it has no fixed shape

geologist a scientist who specializes in the study of a planet's minerals and rocks

glacier a slowly moving mass of ice

global warming the gradual increase in the temperature of Earth's atmosphere

hardness a mineral property described by how easily the mineral can scratch something else or be scratched itself

humus a material that forms from decayed plants and animals

igneous rock the type of rock that forms when magma or lava cools

intrusive rock a type of igneous rock that forms when magma hardens below Earth's surface

lava hot molten rock, or magma, that erupts from a volcano

liquid a substance in which the particles are loosely held together so that the substance can flow

magma a layer of hot, melted rock found below Earth's crust

metallic having the property of a metal, such as being shiny and a good conductor of electricity

metamorphic rock rock that has changed from one type of rock to another

mineral a substance with a definite chemical composition and crystal structure found naturally in the ground

mineral vein a mineral that has formed in cracks in rocks and so is found in thin layers

mining removing metals or minerals from the ground

molecule particle made from two or more atoms joined together

nutrient a substance that plants use to grow healthy and strong

ore a rock that contains a metal or a valuable mineral

organic rock rock formed from the remains of living things

particles very tiny pieces of a substance

property a particular feature of a mineral or chemical

resource something that can be used by people and so is considered valuable

rock cycle the never-ending cycle in which rocks build, break down, and re-form

sediment small, loose pieces of material that come from rocks, minerals, and living things

sedimentary rock rock formed by layers of sediment that are pressed and then stick together

silt a type of sediment of mud or clay that is found at the bottom of a river or lake

soil a mixture of rock particles, minerals, air, water, and the decayed remains of living things

soil horizon a horizontal layer of soil or subsoil

solid a substance in which the particles are strongly held together so that the substance has a fixed shape

solution a fluid with a substance dissolved in it

splint something that is strapped to a broken limb to hold it in place

streak a property of a mineral described by the color of the mineral's powder left behind when the mineral is scraped against a special, unglazed tile

subsoil layer of soil beneath topsoil formed from clay mixed with other materials that have washed down from the topsoil

texture property of soil described by the particle size of materials in the soil such as clay and sand

topsoil the top layer of soil made of a crumbly, dark mixture of clay, sand, silt, decayed organic material, and minerals

ultraviolet light light that cannot be seen by human eyes. It causes certain materials to glow.

weathering the process of rocks breaking down through the action of natural processes, such as wind, rain, ice, snow, and plant roots

Find Out More

Books

Cooper, John. *Planet Earth and Art Activities*. NY: Crabtree Press, 2002.

Dayton, Connor. *Crystals*. NY: Rosen Publishing, 2007.

Faulkner, Rebecca. *Geology Rocks! Series*. Chicago: Heinemann-Raintree, 2008 .

Fuller, Sue. *1001 Facts About Rocks and Minerals*. NY: DK Publishing, 2002.

Hantula, Richard. *Rocks and Fossils*. Pleasantville, NY: Gareth Stevens, 2007.

Sheen, Martin. *Rocks and Minerals*. NY: DK Publishing, 2008.

Websites

http://www.rocksforkids.com/RFK/howrocks.html
A kid-friendly site that will introduce you to the adventure of Earth Science from discovering Earth's crust all the way through rock-hunting and even birthstones!

http://terraweb.wr.usgs.gov/TRS/kids/
The TerraWeb site from the U.S. Geological Survey has great links to everything related to geology and the Earth.

http://www.bgs.ac.uk/education/resources.html
A site hosted by the British Geological Survey with links to all types of interesting sites including the story of how a student turned her love of rocks into her own museum.

Answers

Page 19 : magnetite

Page 44 : **1.** b **2.** d **3.** a **4.** c **5.** a **6.** a **7.** c **8.** d **9.** b **10.** a

Index